Mr. Ha Ha

By Joy Cowley

Illustrated by Elizabeth Sawyer

Dominie Press, Inc.

Publisher: Christine Yuen
Editor: John S. F. Graham
Designer: Lois Stanfield
Illustrator: Elizabeth Sawyer

Published by:

🝱 **Dominie Press, Inc.**

1949 Kellogg Avenue
Carlsbad, California 92008 USA

www.dominie.com

Paperback ISBN 0-7685-1073-2
Library Bound Edition ISBN 0-7685-1488-6
Printed in Singapore by PH Productions Pte Ltd
1 2 3 4 5 6 PH 04 03 02

Table of Contents

Chapter One
A Different Uniform 4

Chapter Two
A Good Laugh 6

Chapter Three
A Really Big Problem 9

Chapter Four
Something Has to Be Done 12

Chapter Five
Mr. Boo Hoo 15

Chapter Six
In Plain Clothes 21

Chapter One

A Different Uniform

During the week,
Jed's dad drove a bus.
He wore a blue uniform
and took people
all over town.

But on the weekends
he often wore
a different uniform.
It was all crazy colors,
and it had big shoes
and an orange wig.

Yes, some weekends,
Jed's dad was a clown
called Mr. Ha Ha.

Chapter Two

A Good Laugh

Jed liked to watch
his dad at children's parties.

"Here comes Mr. Ha Ha!"
the children would scream,
jumping up and down.

Mr. Ha Ha could juggle
two cups, a coffee pot,
and a toy octopus.

He could turn his hat
into a watering can.
When he watered his jacket,
big yellow sunflowers
grew out of its pockets.

Dad said to Jed,
"I love making people laugh.
I'll tell you this, Jed.
There aren't many problems
that can't be fixed
with a good laugh."

Chapter Three
A Really Big Problem

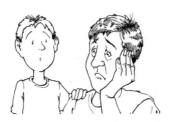

But one day, Jed's dad
had a really big problem.
He lost his job.

"I've been driving those buses
for twenty years," he said.

Jed tried to comfort him.
"You'll get another job."

His dad shook his head.
"I don't want another job.
I want my old job back."

For days,
Jed's dad stayed in the house.
He didn't shave
or change his clothes.
He hardly ate anything.
He just sat in front of the TV,
drinking coffee and looking sad.

Chapter Four

Something Has to Be Done

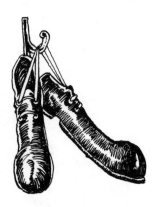

On Saturday, Jed said, "Hey, Dad! Isn't Mr. Ha Ha going to a party today?"

"I've canceled," said his dad. "I'm tired of clowning around."

Jed hugged his dad.
"I thought you said laughter
could fix any problem."

His dad grunted.
"I was wrong," he said.

Jed stepped back
and scratched his head.
Something had to be done
about his sad father.

He went upstairs
to his dad's room
and opened a drawer.
Yes, there it was.
The clown makeup box.

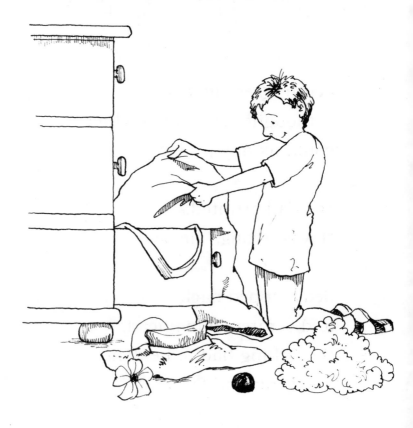

Chapter Five

Mr. Boo Hoo

Jed came downstairs
dressed in the clown suit.
He tripped and fell down
the last five steps.

His father jumped up.
"What the heck are you doing?"

Jed said, "Knock, knock."

"Who's there?" said his dad.

"Oscar," said Jed,
getting to his feet.

"Oscar who?" his dad asked.

"Oscar silly question
and you get a silly answer,"
Jed said. "Ha ha ha."

There was a small smile
on his father's face.
"Are you trying to cheer me up?"

"Watch this!" said Jed.
And he began to juggle
two cups, the coffee pot,
and the toy octopus.

The cups and the coffee pot
smashed on the floor,
and the octopus landed
on Jed's head.

"It's the first time
I've juggled," said Jed.

Now his dad was laughing.
"All right. I get the point.
I've been an old sourpuss,
haven't I?"

"Put it this way," Jed replied.
"You've been Mr. Boo Hoo,
not Mr. Ha Ha."

Dad put his arm around Jed.
"I'd better become Mr. Ha Ha again,
before you smash all my gear."

Chapter Six

In Plain Clothes

The next week, Jed's dad went out to look for work.

He got a job driving a taxi.

He said to Jed,
"Son, you've taught me
an important thing.
When people are sad,
they need someone
to cheer them up."

Jed said, "Wow, Dad!
That's deep thinking.
Does this mean
you'll be Mr. Ha Ha
in plain clothes,
when you're driving
the taxi?"

"Something like that,"
said his father.

Jed grinned.

"I'll tell you this, Dad.

There aren't many problems

that can't be fixed

with a good laugh."